OXFORD
UNIVERSITY PRESS

Oxford International Primary History

Helen Crawford

1

Oxford International Primary for enquiring minds

OXFORD

OXFORD
UNIVERSITY PRESS

Great Clarendon Street, Oxford, OX2 6DP, United Kingdom

Oxford University Press is a department of the University of Oxford. It furthers the University's objective of excellence in research, scholarship, and education by publishing worldwide. Oxford is a registered trade mark of Oxford University Press in the UK and in certain other countries.

British Library Cataloguing in Publication Data
Data available

ISBN 978-0-19-841809-2

7 9 10 8 6

Paper used in the production of this book is a natural, recyclable product made from wood grown in sustainable forests. The manufacturing process conforms to the environmental regulations of the country of origin.

Printed in India by Multivista Global Pvt. Ltd

Acknowledgements

Cover: Carlo Molinari

Artwork: Aptara

Photos: p19 (TL): knyazevfoto/Shutterstock; **p19 (TM):** David Papazian/Shutterstock; **p19 (TR):** ATAHAC/Shutterstock; **p19 (ML):** Petr Nad/Shutterstock; **p19 (MC):** Khaled ElAdawy/Shutterstock; **p19 (MR):** David Papazian/Shutterstock; **p19 (BL):** Charles Harker/Shutterstock; **p19 (BM):** Jodie Johnson/Shutterstock; **p19 (BR):** mubus7/Shutterstock; **p22 (TL) & p32 (L):** TasfotoNL/Shutterstock; **p22 (TR):** Hung Chung Chih/Shutterstock; **p22 (BL):** Andrew Lam/Shutterstock; **p22 (BR) & p32 (R):** Andrew Roland/Shutterstock; **p23:** Emma Durnford/Alamy; **p26 (T):** PhotosIndia.com LLC/Alamy; **p26 (M):** Alexandra Lande/Shutterstock; **p26 (B):** Lamp with a handle with a horse head, from the burial mound of Mikri Doxipara Zoni, near Kyprinos, Greece (bronze), Roman, (2nd century AD)/Private Collection/Bildarchiv Steffens/Prof. Ulrich Schendzielorz/Bridgeman Images; **p27 (L):** Panther Media GmbH/Alamy; **p27 (R):** Electric filament, 1879 (glass & wood) (see also 3197 & 259549-50), Edison, Thomas Alva (1847-1931)/Science Museum, London, UK/Bridgeman Images; **p28 (L):** frazaz/iStockphoto; p28 (R): Heritage Image Partnership Ltd / Alamy Stock Photo; **p29:** (c)Maurice Collins Images Collection /Mary Evans Picture Library; **p31 (L) & p33 (L):** Bjorn Heller/Shutterstock; **p31 (M):** Volodymyr Krasyuk/Shutterstock; **p31 (R) & p33 (R):** Piotr Adamowicz/Shutterstock; **p34-p35:** TeaGraphicDesign/Shutterstock; **p40:** Anton Rogozin/Shutterstock; **p41:** Granger Historical Picture Archive/Alamy; **p44 (TL):** Laborant/Shutterstock; **p44 (TR):** Yvan Travert/akg-images; **p44 (BL):** Gts/Shutterstock; **p44 (BR):** Charlesimage; **p45 (L):** Casper1774 Studio/Shutterstock; **p45 (R):** Afp/Getty

Although we have made every effort to trace and contact all copyright holders before publication this has not been possible in all cases. If notified, the publisher will rectify any errors or omissions at the earliest opportunity.

Contents

In this unit you will:

- talk about history as a study of the past
- describe how you have changed over time
- describe how you have stayed the same
- talk about how you are similar to and different from other people

History is the study of what happened in the past. **The past** is all the time before now. Your history is the story of all the things that have happened to you and your family in the past. Everybody has a different history.

? Look at the pictures. The pictures show how Ahmed has changed since he was a baby. What can you see? Can you point to the pictures in order from when Ahmed was youngest to oldest? Can you explain why you have chosen this order?

1.1 All about me!

We are all different from each other. Read about Mia and Ahmed. How are they different from you? How are they similar to you?

Let's meet Mia

Hello, my name is Mia. I am 6 years old. I was born in September.

I have one brother, Adam. Adam is 9 years old. Adam is older than me.

I like riding my bicycle and I like drawing pictures.

Let's meet Ahmed

Hello, my name is Ahmed.
I am 5 years old.
I was born in May.

I have one sister, Laila.
Laila is 2 years old.
Laila is younger than me.

I like playing basketball and I like reading books.

Activities

1 Choose Mia or Ahmed. Write how you are similar to and different from the person you have chosen.

2 Draw a number line showing ages from 1 year old to 10 years old.

   a Write Mia, Adam, Ahmed and Laila in the correct places on the number line.

   b How old are you? Write your name in the correct place on the number line.

   c Who is the oldest? Who is the youngest?

Challenge

Talk to a friend. Find out all the ways you are similar to and different from each other.

1.2 When I was a baby

We change as we grow older. How has Mia changed since she was a baby? How has she stayed the same?

Mia today

Look at this picture of Mia. She is riding her bicycle.

Mia as a baby

Now look at this picture. It shows Mia when she was a baby.

Talk to your friends. How was Mia different when she was a baby?

When we were babies we ate different food from the food we eat now. We played with different toys. We wore different clothes.

Mia has changed since she was a baby. But Mia is still the same person.

Talk to your friends. How has Mia stayed the same?

Activities

1 Write about all the ways you have changed since you were a baby. Write about how you have stayed the same.

2 Bring to school a photo of yourself as a baby. Make a class display. Look at all the different photos.

   a How have your friends changed?

   b How have they stayed the same?

Challenge

Write a caption for your baby photo. Add your caption to the class display.

1.3 My timeline

A timeline is a way of showing when something happened in the past. A timeline helps us to put what happened in the correct order.

Ahmed's timeline

Ahmed has written a **timeline**.

Ahmed's timeline shows different events in his life. The timeline begins when Ahmed was born.

Word

event something important that happens

> 0 years – I was born.
>
> 1 year – I walked.
>
> 2 years – I kicked a ball.
>
> 3 years – My sister Laila was born.
>
> 4 years – I wrote my name.
>
> 5 years – I went to school.

Activities

1 Follow these instructions to draw a timeline.

   a Draw a line pointing down, like Ahmed's.

   b Write on the timeline different events in your life.

2 We are all different. Our timelines are also different. Look at your friend's timeline.

   a How is it different from your timeline?

   b How is it similar?

Challenge

What events do you think will be on your timeline as you get older? Tell a friend your ideas.

1 My history

A family is a group of people who are related to each other. Our families include our parents, sisters, brothers, grandparents, aunts, uncles and cousins. Everybody has a family.

Different families

Every family is different. Some members of our family live with us. Some members of our family live in different places. Talk to your friends. Tell them about your family.

Mia's family

Mia lives with her brother Adam, her mother, her father and her grandmother.

Different generations

Families are made up of different **generations**. A generation is all the people who are a similar age. Mia and Adam are from one generation. Their mother and father are from a different generation.

A family tree

A **family tree** shows how people in a family are related to each other. Each part of the tree shows a different generation. This family tree shows the different generations who live in Mia's house.

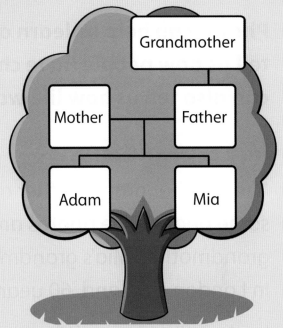

Mia's family tree

Activities

1 Look at the picture of Mia's family. Point to each person and match him or her to the correct name on Mia's family tree.

2 Draw your family tree. How many boxes do you need for the people in each generation? Label each person with his or her name.

Challenge

How is your family tree different from Mia's? How is it the same? Tell a friend.

1.5 What can we learn from a photo?

Photos can help us learn about the past. Photos can tell us how people have changed over time. Photos can also tell us how life was different in the past.

Mia's grandmother

Mia and her grandmother are looking at some photos. The photos are of Mia's grandmother. Mia's grandmother was born in London, England, 60 years ago.

Look at the photos. What can you see?

What do the photos tell you about Mia's grandmother and her life?

Life in the past

This is what Mia's grandmother tells Mia about the photos.

This was 30 years ago. I was working in an office in London. This was my first computer.

This was 60 years ago. I was sleeping in my pram. The pram was different from the baby buggies we have today.

This was 50 years ago. I was at school. We sat at wooden desks. The teacher wrote on a blackboard with chalk.

This was six years ago. You were a small baby then, Mia.

Activities

1 Work with a friend. Look at the photos of Mia's grandmother. Read the speech bubbles. Can you match each speech bubble to the correct photo?

2 Look at the photo of the computer. What can you see? How is it different from the computers we use today? Write down your ideas.

Challenge

Some of the photos are black and white. Some of the photos are colour. Can you use the Internet or ask an adult to find out why?

Answer these questions in your notebook.

Choose the best answer from the choices below.
Write a, b or c as your answer.

1   When we compare two or more things, we look at
     what is similar and what is:

     a   newer

     b   different

     c   older

2   The past is:

     a   the time before now

     b   the world around us

     c   the time now

3   All the people who are a similar age are called a:

   a   family

   b   generation

   c   timeline

4   We can show how people in a family are related to each other on a:

   a   photo

   b   timeline

   c   family tree

Decide if these statements are true or false. Write 'True' or 'False' for each one.

5   A timeline is a line that shows when events happened in the past.

6   Every family is the same.

7   Photos can tell us what life was like in the past.

Now complete these tasks.

8   Write the name of someone who is in the same generation as you.

9   Write the name of someone who is in a different generation from you.

10 Write three ways you have changed since you were a baby. Write three ways you have stayed the same.

2 What were houses like long ago?

In this unit you will:

- compare old and modern houses
- order household objects on a timeline
- describe how houses have changed over time

In the past, houses were not the same as the houses we live in today. Houses looked different on the outside. The rooms inside were different. Houses were different in different parts of the world. What were houses like long ago?

> **modern invention**

? Look at the doors in the photographs. They are all different. Which doors are old? Which doors are new? How do you know?

Look at the pictures of different houses. Some of the houses are old. Some of the houses are modern. Modern houses were built in the time we live in now.

Old and modern

This **modern** house is in Dubai.

This house is in China. It is more than 300 years old.

These modern houses are in Singapore. They are called apartments.

This house is in England. It is more than 400 years old.

Word

apartment a set of rooms for living in, usually on one floor of a building

Chimneys

Some houses have a fire to keep the rooms warm. The smoke from the fire goes out of a chimney at the top of the house. Many modern houses have no fireplace and no chimney. Does your house have a chimney?

What can you see?

Look at the pictures on page 20 again. Look at the different parts of the houses. On each house, look for:

- the windows
- the door
- the walls
- the roof
- the chimney.

Activities

1 Look at the pictures. How are the modern houses different from the old houses? How are they similar? Talk to a friend and share your ideas.

2 Write about your house. How is it similar to or different from the houses in the pictures?

Challenge

Collect some pictures of different houses in your local area. Find out when the houses were built. Sort the pictures into two groups: old houses and modern houses. Make a class display.

2.2 In the kitchen

In the kitchen we prepare and cook food. What were kitchens like in the past? How did people cook food long ago?

An old kitchen

Jug

Kettle

Stove

Bellows

Coal bucket

Bowl

Spoon

Table

Look at the picture on page 22. It shows a kitchen in France more than 150 years ago.

What can you see? Can you name the different kitchen objects?

Look at the picture on page 22.

The stove

The stove cooked the food. The kettle on the stove heated the water. The fire heated the stove. The bellows blew air on to the coal fire to make the fire hotter.

Word

bellows a bag that blows out air on to a fire when you squeeze it

Activities

1 Tell a friend about the kitchen in your house.

 a How is it different from the kitchen in the picture?

 b How is food cooked in your kitchen?

 c How is water heated?

2 Write a list of all the objects in the picture. On your list, put a tick next to the objects that are in a modern kitchen.

Challenge

Ask your grandparents how they cooked food in the past. Find out how kitchens have changed over time in your local area.

2 What were houses like long ago?

Lights help us to see when it is dark. Modern houses have electric lights.

What is happening in this picture?

Tell a friend about all the different lights in your house.

Lighting up the past

In the past, houses did not have the electric lights that we have today.

A candle

Some houses were lit by candles. The Ancient Egyptians used candles 5000 years ago.

Some houses were lit by oil lamps. People have used oil lamps for thousands of years.

This Roman oil lamp is 1800 years old.

Some houses were lit by gas lamps. The gas lamp was invented in 1792, about 225 years ago. An **invention** is something new that is made for the very first time.

A gas lamp

Activities

1 Draw a timeline. Write these words in the correct order on the timeline: oil lamp, electric light, candle, gas lamp. Draw a picture of each object.

2 Compare the picture of the first electric light bulb with a modern light bulb. How are the light bulbs similar? How are they different? Tell a friend.

Word

electric electricity is energy that is carried through wires

Challenge

Use the Internet or look in a book to find out who invented the electric light bulb.

In the bathroom we wash and keep clean. How did people wash and keep clean long ago?

Comparing bathrooms

This is a modern bathroom. What can you see?

This is a bathroom in Germany 100 years ago. What can you see?

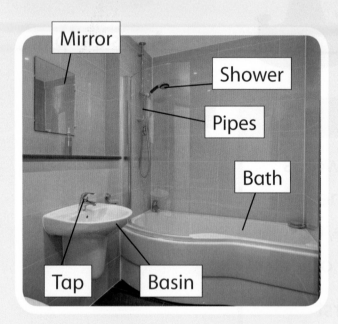

Mirror

Shower

Pipes

Bath

Tap

Basin

What about water?

Pipes bring water into a modern bathroom. We turn on a tap and water comes out.

Be a good historian

Good historians know that some things stay the same over time. What is the same about both bathrooms in the pictures?

Many houses in the past did not have pipes and taps.
People used water from different places.

Some people washed with water from a river.

Some people washed with water from a well.

Some people washed with water from a pump.

In some parts of the world, people still wash with water from a well, from a pump or from a river.

Activities

1. Look at a modern toothpaste advert. How is it similar to and how is it different from the advert on this page? Tell a friend your ideas.

2. Find out how people in your local area collected water in the past. Did people use a river, a well or a pump? How do you know?

Did you know?

Tubes of toothpaste were invented in 1890, more than 125 years ago.

Challenge

Find out how people cleaned their teeth before the invention of toothpaste. Are some of these methods still used today?

2.5 Washing day

Many houses today have a washing machine to clean clothes. How were clothes washed in the past?

Washing clothes

Read the rhyme. Look at the picture.

Washing day

Washing day

Let's all wash the clothes this way

Put the washing in the tub

Use the soap to rub, rub, rub

Up and down with the stick

Up and down quick, quick, quick

Peg the washing on the line

Out to dry in the sunshine

Find:

- the washing tub
- the soap
- the pegs
- the stick
- the washing line
- the jug.

How did people wash clothes in the past?

Ironing clothes

We use an iron to press clothes.

An iron has a handle. The bottom of the iron is made of metal. We make the metal very hot using electricity or coals from a hot fire. We hold the handle and the hot metal presses the clothes.

A coal iron

An old electric iron

A modern electric iron

Activities

1 Work with a friend.

- Learn to say the rhyme.
- Make up some actions to match the words.
- Show the rest of the class.

2 How have irons changed over time? How have irons stayed the same? Write your ideas.

Challenge

Find out how people washed and ironed clothes when your grandparents were children. What has changed? What has stayed the same?

② Review

Answer these questions in your notebook.

Choose the best answer from the choices below.
Write a, b or c as your answer.

1   A modern house is from:

    a   the time we live in now

    b   a long time ago

    c   the past

2   An invention is something new that is:

    a   made by many people

    b   made for the first time

    c   made of many materials

3   Thousands of years ago, people used:

    a   gas lamps

    b   electric lights

    c   oil lamps and candles

4 A chimney:

    a washes clothes

    b takes the smoke from a fire outside the house

    c cooks food

5 The electric light bulb was invented about:

    a 14 years ago

    b 140 years ago

    c 1400 years ago

Decide if these statements are true or false.
Write 'True' or 'False' for each one.

6 The kitchen stove cooked food and heated water.

7 In a modern bathroom water comes out of a well.

8 Electricity is energy that is carried through wires.

Now complete these tasks.

9 Compare a coal iron and an electric iron. Write one way they are different. Write one way they are similar.

10 Write three ways houses have stayed the same over time. Write three ways houses have changed.

3 Three brave explorers

In this unit you will:

- describe the lives of three explorers
- compare three different explorers
- talk about different ways we remember the past

I lived 700 years ago. I lived in the 14th century.

I lived 600 years ago. I lived in the 15th century.

Christopher Columbus

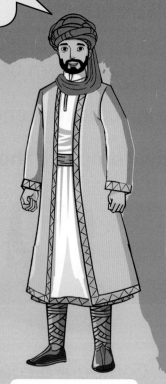

Ibn Battuta

14th century	15th century	16th century	17th centur

An **explorer** is someone who goes on a journey to learn about new people and places. Who explored the world in the past? Where did they go? How did they travel? What did they see?

explorer
century
voyage

Edmund Hillary

I was born 100 years ago. I was born in the 20th century.

? A **century** is 100 years. Look at the timeline. Find the century when each explorer lived. Which century do we live in now? Find it on the timeline.

18th century	19th century	20th century	21st century

Ibn Battuta was an explorer. Ibn Battuta was born in Morocco. He lived 700 years ago in the 14th century.

Can you find Morocco on the map?

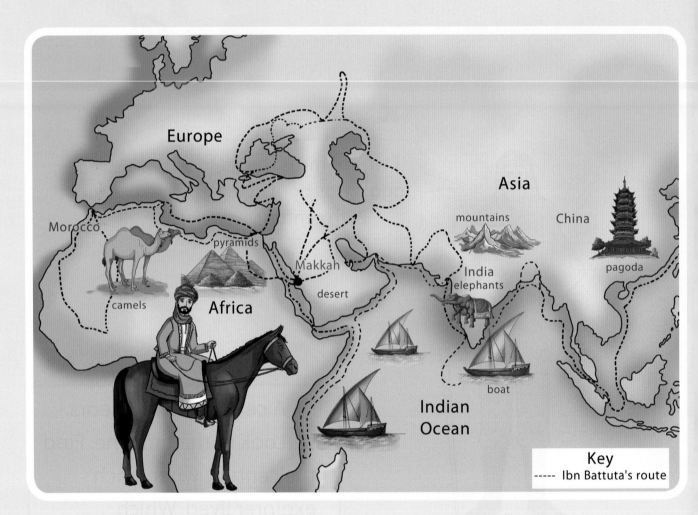

Where did Ibn Battuta travel?

Ibn Battuta travelled from Morocco to Makkah as a pilgrim. A pilgrim is someone who travels to a holy place.

Ibn Battuta travelled for many years. He went to Asia, India and China. He went to Europe. He went to Africa. He travelled across deserts, mountains and oceans.

Why did Ibn Battuta travel?

Ibn Battuta wanted to learn about different people and places in the world.

How did Ibn Battuta travel?

Ibn Battuta rode on horses, camels and elephants. He sailed on boats.

How do we know about Ibn Battuta?

Ibn Battuta wrote a book about all the places he visited. The book is called *Rihla*. This means 'journey'.

Activities

1 Look at the map. With a friend, find all the places that Ibn Battuta visited.

2 Look at the map. Write a list of the things that Ibn Battuta saw on his travels.

Challenge

Ibn Battuta wrote a book called *Rihla*. Design a front cover for *Rihla*.

Christopher Columbus was a sailor. He was born in Italy. He lived 600 years ago in the 15th century.

Can you find Italy on the map?

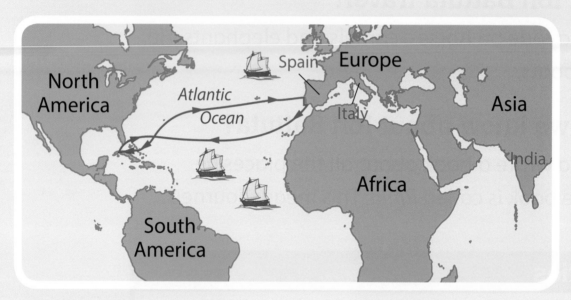

A voyage

In 1492 Christopher Columbus sailed from Europe across the Atlantic Ocean. He wanted to find a new way to sail to India. The King and Queen of Spain gave him money for the **voyage**.
A voyage is a long journey.

Columbus sailed with 90 sailors and 3 ships. The voyage took a long time. There was little food and water. The sailors were scared.

Land ahoy!

After 70 days, the sailors saw land. Columbus thought it was India. But it was not India. It was a new land – America.

Columbus did not discover America. People were already living there.

Columbus returns

Columbus sailed back to Spain. He gave the king and queen a pineapple and a turkey from America.

Columbus sailed to America three more times. Other explorers also sailed to America.

Did you know?

Columbus was not the first person from Europe to travel to America. Viking explorers sailed to America 500 years before him.

Activities

1 What do you think Columbus said when he saw land?

  a Draw a picture of Columbus on a ship.

  b Write what you think he said in a speech bubble.

2 Why do you think Columbus gave the king and queen a pineapple and a turkey? Explain your ideas to a friend.

Words

sailor a person who works on a boat or ship

discover to find or see something for the first time

Challenge

Look at a globe. Find: Europe, India, America.

Edmund Hillary was an explorer and mountain climber. He was born in New Zealand. He was born about 100 years ago.

Can you find New Zealand on the map?

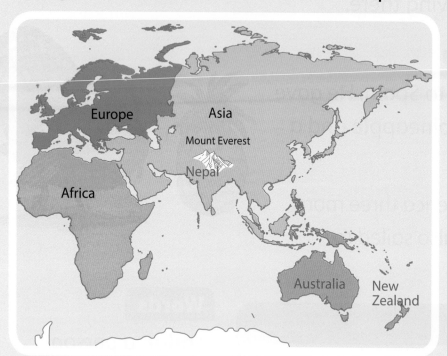

Mount Everest

Mount Everest is the highest mountain in the world.

Can you find Mount Everest on the map?

Edmund Hillary wanted to climb to the top of Mount Everest. Nobody had ever climbed to the top before.

Did you know?

Mount Everest is nearly 11 times higher than the Burj Khalifa, the world's tallest building!

Journey to the top

In 1953 Edmund Hillary met Tenzing Norgay. Tenzing Norgay was a mountain guide from Nepal.

The two men started to climb Mount Everest. They climbed higher and higher.

There was snow and ice on the mountain. It was very cold and very dangerous.

At last, they climbed to the top. Hillary and Norgay were famous because they were the first people to climb to the top of Mount Everest.

Edmund Hillary and Tenzing Norgay

More adventures

Edmund Hillary wanted more adventures.

He travelled to the coldest places in the world. First, he travelled to the South Pole. Then he travelled to the North Pole.

Challenge

Find out three facts about Hillary's adventures to the North Pole **or** the South Pole.

Activities

1 Work with a friend. One of you is a television reporter. One of you is Edmund Hillary. Make up a television interview about the climb to the top of Mount Everest.

2 Imagine you are Edmund Hillary. Write some sentences for your diary. Describe the day you reached the top of Mount Everest.

3.4 Who was the bravest explorer?

Mia, Ahmed and Jamal are comparing the three explorers. Which explorer was the bravest?

Ibn Battuta

Mia says Ibn Battuta was the bravest explorer.

> Ibn Battuta was very brave.
>
> He travelled for many years.
>
> He travelled to many places, far from home.
>
> He travelled across deserts, mountains and oceans.

Christopher Columbus

Ahmed says Christopher Columbus was the bravest explorer.

> Christopher Columbus was very brave.
>
> He tried to find a new way to sail around the world.
>
> He sailed across the Atlantic Ocean.
>
> He sailed to a new land far away.

Edmund Hillary

Jamal says Edmund Hillary was the bravest explorer.

Edmund Hillary was very brave.
He climbed dangerous mountains.
He climbed in snow and ice.
He climbed to the top of Mount Everest.

Activities

1 Which explorer do you think was the bravest? Tell your friends why you think this.

2 Make a class display comparing the three explorers. Show on the display how they are similar to each other and how they are different from each other.

Challenge

Have a class vote to find out which explorer your class thinks was the bravest. Show the results on a pictogram. Add the pictogram to your class display.

3.5 Remembering the three explorers

Ibn Battuta, Christopher Columbus and Edmund Hillary were famous explorers. They lived in the past. Today we still remember them.

Ibn Battuta

This is the Ibn Battuta shopping centre in Dubai. The shopping centre is named after Ibn Battuta.

This figure of Ibn Battuta is in China.

Christopher Columbus

Colombia is a country in South America. Colombia is named after Christopher Columbus.

This stamp is from Italy. It shows a picture of Christopher Columbus.

Edmund Hillary

This is a bank note from New Zealand. There is a picture of Edmund Hillary on the bank note.

Be a good historian

Good historians know that we remember people from the past in different ways. In how many different ways do we remember the three explorers?

This part of Mount Everest was called Hillary's Step. It was named after Edmund Hillary.

Activities

1 Look at the pictures. Write a list of all the different ways we remember the three explorers.

2 Look at the money you use in your country.

   a Can you see a picture of a person?

   b Write the name of this person.

   c Write three facts about this person.

Challenge

Find out about a famous person who lived in your local area.

How do we remember this person today?

③ Review

Answer these questions in your notebook.

Choose the best answer from the choices below.
Write a, b or c as your answer.

1   A century is:

    a   10 years

    b   100 years

    c   200 years

2   We live in the:

    a   14th century

    b   20th century

    c   21st century

3   Ibn Battuta was born in:

    a   China

    b   India

    c   Morocco

4   Christopher Columbus sailed from
Europe to America across the:

    a   Atlantic Ocean

    b   Indian Ocean

    c   Pacific Ocean

5 Edmund Hillary was the first person to climb:

  a Mount Zealand

  b Mount Norgay

  c Mount Everest

**Decide if these statements are true or false.
Write 'True' or 'False' for each one.**

6 A voyage is a long journey.

7 Ibn Battuta wrote a book called *Rihla*.
Rihla means 'famous'.

8 When Christopher Columbus discovered
America, people were already living there.

Now complete these tasks.

9 Compare Ibn Battuta, Christopher Columbus and
Edmund Hillary. Write one way they are all similar.
Write one way they are all different.

10 Who do you think was the
most important explorer?
Write a sentence to explain
your ideas.

Christopher Columbus was very
brave.
He tried to find a new way to sail
around the world.
He sailed across the Atlantic Ocean.
He sailed to a new land far away.

Ibn Battuta was very brave.
He travelled for many years.
He travelled to many places, far
from home.
He travelled across deserts,
mountains and oceans.

Edmund Hillary was very brave.
He climbed dangerous mountains.
He climbed in snow and ice.
He climbed to the top of Mount
Everest.

Vocabulary quiz

Answer these questions in your notebook.

1 My history

1 Match the words from the box with the pictures.

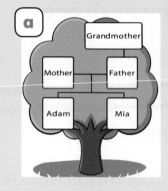

> a family tree
> a timeline

2 Match the words from the box with the definitions.

   a all the members of a family who are of a similar age

   b the study of what happened in the past

   c all the time before now

   d something important that happens.

> history   the past   generation   event

2 What were houses like long ago?

1 Match the words from the box with the pictures.

> apartments
> a house

2 Match the words from the box with the definitions.

a a set of rooms for living in, usually on one floor of a building

b from the time we live in now

c energy that is carried through wires

d something new, made for the first time

| modern   invention   apartment   electricity |

3 Three brave explorers

1 What does this picture show?

| a map   a book |

2 Match the words from the box with the definitions.

a an exciting or dangerous journey

b one hundred years

c to find or see something for the first time

d someone who goes on a journey to learn about new people and places

e a person that many people know

f a long journey

| explorer   century   voyage
discover   famous   adventure |

Glossary

adventure an exciting or dangerous journey

apartment a set of rooms for living in, usually on one floor of a building

bellows a bag that blows out air on to a fire when you squeeze it

century one hundred years

discover to find or see something for the first time

electric electricity is energy that is carried through wires

event something important that happens

explorer someone who goes on a journey to learn about new people and places

family tree a way of showing how people in a family are related to each other

famous a person that many people know

generation all the members of a family who are of a similar age

history the study of what happened in the past

invention something new, made for the first time

modern from the time we live in now

sailor a person who works on a boat or ship

the past all the time before now

timeline a way of showing events in order of when they happened, along a line

voyage a long journey